Dolley Madison

Dolley Madison

By Patricia Ryon Quiri

Franklin Watts
New York / Chicago / London / Sydney
A First Book

Photographs copyright ©: National Portrait Gallery, Washington, 2; Virginia State Library and Archives, 10, 28, 38; The Bettmann Archive, 12, 51; North Wind Picture Archives, 14, 27 (left, center, right), 33, 45; Library of Congress, 18, 26, 49 (bottom), 55; New York Public Library Picture Collection, 20, 41, 47, 49 (top), 59; The New-York Historical Society, 24, 25; Stock Montage, Inc., 31; Colonial Williamsburg Foundation, 35; White House Historical Association, 43, 44; National Trust for Historical Preservation, 53.

Library of Congress Cataloging-in-Publication Data

Quiri, Patricia Ryon.
Dolley Madison / by Patricia Ryon Quiri.
p. cm.—(First books)
Includes bibliographical references and index.
Summary: A biography of the popular wife of President James Madison.
ISBN 0-531-20097-3 (HC, library binding)
1. Madison, Dolley, 1768–1849—Junvenile literature. 2. Madison, James, 1751–1836—Juvenile literature. 3. Presidents—United States—Biography—Juvenile literature. [1. Madison, Dolley, 1768–1849. 2. First ladies.] I. Title. II. Series.
E342.1.Q56 1993
973.5'1'0922—dc20 [B]
92-28300 CIP AC

DEDICATION

For Johnnie Ryon, Betty Quiri, and Ruth Muir—
in whom each, lives a little Dolley.

With love.

Contents

★ ★ ★ ★ ★

★ ★ ★ ★ ★

CHAPTER ONE

Dolley's Childhood

★ ★ ★ ★ ★

On May 20, 1768, a baby girl was born in Guilford County, North Carolina. The baby was named Dolley. Her parents were John and Mary Payne. Dolley's birth occurred at an exciting time. The American colonies were on the verge of fighting for their independence from Great Britain. A new nation, the United States of America, would be born as a result. The young girl, Dolley Payne, grew up during the Revolution and the founding of a new nation. She saw history in the making, and indeed became part of it. Dolley Payne grew up to become one of the most beloved first ladies in American history.

When Dolley was ten years old, her family moved to Scotchtown, Virginia. They rented a plantation with a large house surrounded by 960 acres (388.5 hectares) where tobacco, wheat, and corn were grown. Dolley loved to explore the fields and woods at Scotchtown. She and her older half-brothers, Walter and William Temple, would often ride their horses together over the land. Dolley delighted in the beauty of nature. She loved the brilliant colors of the flowers, bushes, and trees. The open fields were a great place for Dolley and her brothers to have running races, something she enjoyed doing throughout her life.

Best of all, Dolley thrived on being with people. And there were plenty of people at Scotchtown. In addition to her older brothers, Dolley had several younger siblings—Isaac, Lucy, Anna, Mary, and eventually John. Working on the plantation were about thirty slaves. Some toiled in the fields, while others worked in the main house caring for the children, cleaning the house, and preparing the meals. One special slave was called "Mother Amy." She was an older woman who cared for the Payne children. She loved them, and the children loved her.

*Scotchtown, Virginia, where Dolley's
family moved when she was ten.*

Running a plantation the size of Scotchtown required slave labor, a practice common throughout the South at that time. John and Mary Payne treated their slaves very kindly. They did not really believe in slavery. Dolley's parents believed that all people—men, women, blacks, and whites—were equal. In those days, this was a very liberal viewpoint that was a result of the Paynes' devotion to the Quaker religion, the Religious Society of Friends.

Those who practiced the Quaker religion, which began in England in the 1600s, believed God lived in the hearts of all people. Education was considered very important for boys as well as girls. Material items were considered unimportant. It was the inner soul that mattered, not things. Vanity was considered a sin, so Dolley and her siblings had to wear plain dark clothes—no ruffles, no buckles, no ribbons. They were not allowed to go to parties or dances. This didn't bother Dolley too much. As her mother told her quite often, "things" don't make life happy, people do.

Dolley did, however, admire the many beautiful "things" her Grandmother and Grandfather Payne had. They were not Quakers, and they owned many lovely possessions. What most awed Dolley were Grandmother Payne's gorgeous gowns of silks and

velvets in all different colors. These clothes were so
different from the plain grey dresses Dolley's mother
wore. Grandmother Payne once gave Dolley a pretty
piece of jewelry. So no one would see it, she pinned
it under Dolley's dress. Dolley felt so special. When

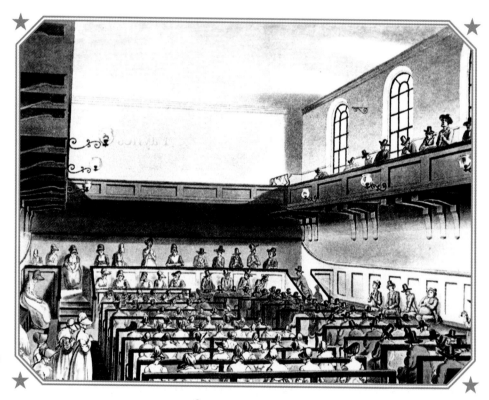

A Quaker Meeting.

she lost the jewelry piece on her way home from school one day, however, she was sure she was being punished for being so vain.

When the American Revolution began, the Paynes were troubled. Quakers did not believe in war. Consequently, they did not support the patriots in their fight for independence from Great Britain. Dolley was only seven years old at the time. Many neighbors accused the Paynes of being Tories, supporters of the British effort to hold on to the American colonies.

At this point, the Paynes made plans to move to Philadelphia, Pennsylvania, the original American home of the Quakers. There, the Paynes felt they could live peacefully and comfortably. Prior to their move, Dolley's parents freed each of their slaves. Mother Amy, however, had no desire to become a free woman. She wanted to move to Philadelphia with the Paynes and continue to care for the children. John and Mary Payne agreed to this under one condition—Mother Amy would get paid for her work.

In July 1783, Dolley's family arrived in the bustling city of Philadelphia. Dolley found that life was quite different in Philadelphia. The Payne home was much smaller than the Scotchtown plantation house and occupied only a small plot of land. No

Busy Philadelphia, where the Paynes moved in 1783.

longer would Dolley and her brothers ride endlessly on horseback through thick woods and over vast fields. Dolley's father was not going to be a farmer anymore. Instead, he turned his attention to business.

City life brought many other changes to Dolley's world. She found the Quakers in Philadelphia were not as strict as those in Virginia. With some reluctance, her mother allowed her to go to parties and picnics with other Quaker friends. Dolley became best friends with a girl named Eliza (Elizabeth) Collins. The two girls enjoyed exploring Philadelphia and its buildings. But most of all, Dolley enjoyed watching the people. She admired the brightly colored clothing. Though she thought these outfits beautiful, she still had to wear her plain grey dress.

It didn't take long before Dolley blossomed into a pretty young woman. She had black hair and lovely blue eyes. Dolley was popular among her peers, and some said she was like "a breath of fresh air" to people. This was because she was truly interested in all sorts of people and did not draw attention to herself.

On May 25, 1787, delegates from all the states with the exception of Rhode Island assembled at the State House in Philadelphia to draw up a new government for the United States. They met in a constitutional convention. This was an exciting time for Dolley and everyone else who lived in Philadelphia. Perhaps they might get to see important statesmen such as George Washington, Benjamin Franklin, Alexander Hamilton, and James Madison, all of whom were there. These men had a tough job ahead of them. James Madison formulated a plan for establishing a federal government with three distinct branches: executive, legislative, and judicial branches that would share power equally. It was Madison who kept the delegates together through four long hot months of debate and who kept daily records of everything that was discussed at the meetings. He later became the author of the Bill of Rights, guarantees of freedom that were added to the new constitution to ensure approval by the states. It was James Madison who would play an important role in Dolley's life, and she in his.

After much disagreement, in June 1788, the Constitution was finally ratified. It had been accepted by at least nine of the thirteen states. That July 4, the citizens of Philadelphia, including Dolley and her family, celebrated the ratification. Horns blew, bells rang, and a huge parade was staged. The celebration lasted all day. The United States of America was born.

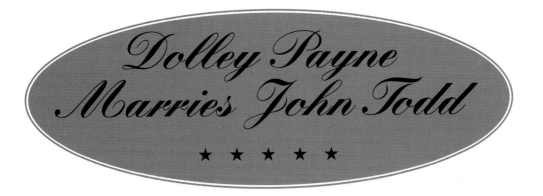

CHAPTER TWO

Dolley Payne Marries John Todd

★ ★ ★ ★ ★

hile the new government was getting underway, Dolley's parents began to have serious financial troubles. Mr. Payne's starch business was doing poorly, and his debts were mounting. Because of these debts, the Society of Friends turned him away.

This was a turning point in Dolley's life. She was twenty-one years old. John Payne had a talk with his daughter about marriage. John Todd, a successful lawyer, was in love with Dolley and wanted to marry

Dolley as a young woman.

her. He had proposed to her before, but Dolley felt she was needed at home. Dolley's father encouraged her to marry Todd, knowing she would be well cared for. On January 7, 1790, Dolley followed her father's advice and married Todd, also a Quaker, in a simple ceremony.

They were a happy couple. His law practice was good, and they enjoyed their involvement with their Quaker meetings. After two years of marriage, they had a son whom they named John Payne Todd. They called him Payne.

Shortly after Payne's birth, Dolley's father died. Dolley visited her mother often. Mrs. Payne ran a boardinghouse to help make ends meet. Her house became well-known among the congressmen who served in the new government now located in Philadelphia. From their frequent visits to Mrs. Payne's boardinghouse, Dolley and John got to know many politicians. Among them was Aaron Burr, the famous senator from New York. The country was very young at this time, and George Washington was the new president.

Much to her delight, Dolley became involved in many social events that took place in Philadelphia, the new capital of the United States. She attended Martha Washington's socials and got to know her well. Dolley also began to wear clothes other than

Martha Washington, the wife of President George Washington, and Dolley's friend.

the traditional Quaker grey. She was very happy and content as her circle of friends grew wider. Dolley loved people and people loved her.

During the summer of 1793, Dolley's fifteen-year-old sister, Lucy, eloped with the President's nephew, George Steptoe Washington. He was not a Quaker, which was disappointing to Dolley's mother. They were young, however, and very happy.

That same summer, Dolley gave birth to another son, William Temple Todd. Shortly after his birth, a yellow fever epidemic hit Philadelphia with ferocity. Yellow fever was a disease that claimed thousands of lives. Doctors didn't know how to treat the disease.

They bled patients so the "bad" blood would flow out, they used medicines such as quinine and camphor, and they used disinfectants such as vinegar and garlic. Nothing worked. More than one hundred years passed before researchers discovered that mosquitoes carried the dreaded disease.

Hundreds of people fled the city of Philadelphia hoping to escape the fatal illness. John Todd took Dolley and the children to the country. Then he went back to the city to help sick people arrange their legal affairs. When his parents became ill with yellow fever, he nursed them both until their deaths. Suddenly, John, too, came down with the disease. He managed to make the trip back into the country to see his beloved Dolley once more. Five days later, on October 24, 1793, John Todd died.

Tragically, Dolley's newborn son also died of what was thought to be an unrelated fever. Grief-stricken, Dolley became very ill. She felt she no longer had a reason to live. Mrs. Payne nursed her through this time. After several days Dolley gradually began to get better.

Dolley had financial worries. John Todd's estate took a long time to settle. His brother was giving Dolley a hard time about her rightful share. Finally, Dolley became so desperate she hired a lawyer to help her. More than a year passed, however, before the estate was settled.

CHAPTER THREE

Dolley and James Madison

★ ★ ★ ★ ★

Dolley decided to move back to Philadelphia with Payne. Her sister Anna, came to live with them. Slowly Dolley became her exuberant self once again. Many men looked at her with admiration, although she was not aware of their interest. Her friendship with Aaron Burr continued, and she asked him to be Payne's legal guardian. It was Aaron Burr who asked Dolley if he could bring James Madison for a visit. This would not be their first meeting, however. As a child, Dolley had met

Madison when he had visited her parents' home many years before.

Dolley sent a note to Eliza Collins in May 1794. The note read, "Thou must come to me. Aaron Burr says that the great little Madison has asked to be brought to see me this evening." And so the courtship began. Madison, a man not much taller than Dolley's own five foot five inch frame, was very serious and quiet. This brilliant man, referred to as "Father of the Constitution," fell in love with Dolley. He was seventeen years older than she. About a month after their first visit, James asked Dolley to marry him. Dolley needed time to consider his proposal. She was a little uncertain of her feelings for him. She respected, admired, and enjoyed his company, but she wasn't sure if she loved him.

Finally she consented. On September 15, 1794, Dolley and James Madison were married at her sister Lucy's home. This marriage ceremony was much different from her first. It was not a Quaker ceremony. Dolley looked radiant in her gown of white satin and ring of orange blossoms that framed her dark hair. Madison wore a black silk coat and intricate lace jabot. (A jabot is a piece of lace or cloth that men wore in the eighteenth century, similar to a necktie.) After the ceremony there was an elaborate meal as well as music and dancing. All in fun, some

girls cut off pieces of Madison's jabot to keep as souvenirs of the wedding. The serious Madison didn't seem to mind this bit of frivolity.

Dolley's respect and admiration for Madison soon grew into true love. James adored Dolley, and shortly after their marriage, he adopted Payne. He was a good father. Dolley doted on her son. In her eyes, he could do no wrong. She gave him anything he wanted, which made him spoiled and demanding. Dolley would never admit to this, however. Payne

*A pencil on ivory sketch of Dolley
Madison by Thomas Christian Lubbers.*

was her only child, as she and James never had children of their own.

In December 1794, Dolley was informed she was no longer a member of the Society of Friends. The Quakers did not approve of her marriage to a non-Quaker. Maybe Dolley was relieved. She could let go of the traditional Quaker way of life, yet still feel the "Inner Light" in her own way. She was free to worship in any way she chose and she was free to dress in any manner she pleased.

This engraving depicts one of Martha Washington's Philadelphia parties.

Back in Philadelphia, Dolley was caught up in a political and social whirlwind. Fridays were reserved for Martha Washington's social gatherings or parties. Here important people discussed politics as well as gossiped. Dolley could talk with anyone, making that person feel like he or she was the most important person in the room. Dolley also learned a lot about politics at these parties.

During this time, there were two political parties in the United States. The Democrat-Republicans (later called the Democrats), led by Thomas Jefferson, believed in power by the people. The Democrat-Republicans represented the farmers and landowners. The Federalists, largely led by Alexander Hamilton, believed the rich should run the country. The Federalists spoke for businessmen and manufacturers. James Madison was a Democrat-Republican.

On March 4, 1797, John Adams, a Federalist, took the oath of office as the second President of the United States. Thomas Jefferson was sworn in as

Left to right: Thomas Jefferson, Alexander Hamilton, John Adams.

*Montpelier, Virginia, James Madison's
family home and plantation.*

Vice-President. Dolley and James were there to watch. All who were there witnessed George Washington's emotional farewell. A new era was about to begin.

With a Federalist as president, James Madison decided to retire from politics. He and Dolley moved to Montpelier with Payne and Dolley's sister, Anna. Montpelier was Madison's family home in Virginia. It was a magnificent plantation where James and his father grew many crops, including tobacco and clover. Dolley did a lot of gardening at Montpelier and assumed the role of hostess at the estate.

Thirty miles from Montpelier was Thomas Jefferson's home, Monticello. Jefferson and Madison were good friends. These two brilliant men wrote each other often and got together whenever the Vice-President was at Monticello. They enjoyed discussing plantation affairs, but inevitably they ended up talking politics and government.

At the time, the United States was having problems with Great Britain and France. These two countries were at war. The Federalists were pro-Great Britain, whereas the Democrat-Republicans sided with France. Great Britain began seizing American ships that were bringing food to France. France, displeased that a Federalist had been elected president, too, began seizing American ships. In short, the United States was in turmoil.

CHAPTER FOUR

Hostess for Thomas Jefferson

★ ★ ★ ★ ★

On March 4, 1801, Thomas Jefferson became the third President of the United States. Aaron Burr was the new Vice-President. The country also had a new capital city, Washington, D.C., which was still under construction. Jefferson selected James Madison as his Secretary of State. Secretaries of State direct U.S relations with other nations. In those days, the office was usually given to the man most likely to be chosen as the next president.

A typical evening party during the nineteenth century.

In May of 1801, the Madisons arrived in Washington, D.C., re-entering political life. Dolley did a lot of entertaining. Because his wife had died, Thomas Jefferson asked Dolley to serve as his official hostess. Dolley proved to be a superior hostess, both at the President's House as well as her own home. She served huge dinners and made sure each guest was attended to and had a good time. Only one person ever had a complaint. Her name was Mrs. Merry, wife of the British minister. She said Dolley's beautiful meal was more like a "harvest home" supper than a meal hosted by a Secretary of State. Dolley's pleasant response was something like, "Why not? It shows how prosperous our country is."

Though Dolley was busy entertaining for Jefferson and Madison, the realization that her family was growing up and moving away saddened her. Payne was eleven years old and was sent off to boarding school. He was enrolled in Alexandria Academy, located across the Potomac River. That winter Dolley's sister, Anna, became engaged to a congressman from Massachusetts named Richard Cutts. She, too, would be moving.

Less than four months after Anna's wedding, a horrible tragedy shook the country. Vice-President Aaron Burr shot and killed Alexander Hamilton in a gun duel. The two men had never liked each other and Hamilton had said many things about Burr that made Burr very angry. Hamilton led the move to prevent Burr from becoming president when Burr and Jefferson received the same number of votes for the presidency. Thanks to Hamilton's influence, Jefferson became president, and Burr, vice-president.

Hamilton, a leading statesman and the first Secretary of the Treasury in Washington, consented to the duel thinking it would save each man's honor. He didn't think harm would come to either of them.

The Hamilton-Burr duel.

The duel took place in Weehawken, New Jersey, just across the Hudson River from New York City. Hamilton fired his gun into the air, while Burr deliberately shot to kill Hamilton. Dolley and James were shocked, as was the entire country. Aaron Burr had once been her friend and the guardian to her son. The country now mourned Hamilton and called Aaron Burr a "cold-blooded murderer." After the duel, Burr became an outlaw and a renegade, trying to get Western colonists to rebel.

CHAPTER FIVE

The Lady Presidentress

★ ★ ★ ★ ★

On March 4, 1809, James Madison was sworn in as the fourth President of the United States. Dolley was the first woman to watch her husband's swearing in. For the occasion she wore a white cotton gown with a long train, and a purple and white bonnet adorned with feathers. Those in attendance strained to get a glimpse of Dolley. That evening at Long's Hotel, an inaugural ball was held. This was the first ball since George Washington's inauguration. Dolley wore a light yellow velvet gown, again with a long train. She also enjoyed wearing outrageous turbans. The one she wore for the ball included two bird of paradise feathers.

As always, Dolley was a most gracious hostess to her nearly four hundred guests. Being friendly, as well as politically minded, she remembered people's names and made appropriate personal remarks to her guests. She was a perfect asset to Madison, whose

James Madison, fourth president of the United States.

health was rather frail, and who did not like parties and the endless standing and handshaking.

One of Dolley's first jobs as the new "Lady Presidentress" (wives of Presidents were not yet called first ladies) was to furnish the President's House. When Madison became president, Jefferson took his belongings back to Monticello. Dolley had a great time decorating. Congress had allotted money for the furnishings because it had decided that the items would belong to the house and remain there. Dolley ordered new curtains in red velvet and yellow satin. Mirrors, though very expensive, were hung to make the rooms look larger. Portraits of Washington, Adams, and Jefferson were hung on the walls of the dining room. Thirty servants were hired as Dolley intended to play a visible role as the President's wife and entertain often.

On Wednesday, March 30, 1809, Dolley gave her first reception. It was open to the public, as would be all subsequent Wednesday evening receptions. At these receptions statesmen had the opportunity to speak to Madison about political matters. Dolley wanted her social gatherings to be informal. She wanted people to mingle, eat, talk, and play cards. These receptions were very different from those of her predecessors, Martha Washington and Abigail Adams. Their parties had been for a very select group and were quite formal. Unlike them, Dolley walked around and chatted with each guest. She carried around a gold box filled with snuff, which she offered to her guests. Although using snuff was not considered appropriate for women, Dolley was known to take a pinch now and then. Some accounts say that she shared her snuff with Madison's political opponents, often breaking the ice between them. Another thing Dolley frequently carried around was the book *Don Quixote*. She was an avid reader, and she felt the book would serve as a conversation piece.

About two hundred guests came to the first reception, which proved to be very successful. The women wore their finest low-cut gowns with ruffles and feathers. Dolley, who now loved wearing beautiful dresses, favored the Empire style. These gowns were cut quite low in front and had short sleeves or no sleeves at all. Her turbans were of silk or satin— some with feathers, others with flowers. Before long, Dolley was known as the best-dressed woman in Washington. People everywhere wanted to know what Mrs. Madison wore and what Mrs. Madison served.

At her socials and dinner parties, Dolley's guests were always treated to delicious American foods, such as fried chicken, New England clam chowder, and smoked ham. She also served delicious

*Dolley's love of high fashion and her refined
style are seen in this portrait.*

sweets. In fact, Dolley was the first to serve "ice creams" in the President's House. This cooling treat had been introduced to her by Thomas Jefferson.

Dolley was an excellent hostess and always enjoyed a party. These parties, however, also served as a political vehicle for her. She used these social occasions to further Madison's political advantage. Because he was shy and retiring in public, it was Dolley who listened to, talked with, and joked among statesmen who were dissatisfied with Madison.

At their dinner parties, Madison always sat Dolley next to the key statesman. Because she was so personable and tactful, it was she who could influence a political figure to take into account Madison's views. Dolley was responsible for much of Madison's popularity and many people credited her for his re-election. During his administration and their marriage, Madison treated Dolley as an equal partner. He shared political information and secrets with her which Dolley always kept to herself. This shared knowledge, however, made Dolley influential in Madison's administration. She was instrumental in the appointments of many government jobs.

Dolley also gave parties for women only. She would invite certain wives of the Cabinet, Senate, and House of Representatives. The conversation always drifted toward politics. It was at these parties that

Dolley could obtain information from the women on where their husbands stood on many political issues. To further political support for Madison, Dolley made it her business to visit the families of new congressmen when they moved to Washington. This often took all day as the number of people who moved to the city increased steadily. Traveling by carriage over the city's unpaved roads was an exhausting undertaking. Dolley, however, knew it was politically important for Madison. She gave her husband's enemies the same warm attention that she gave his friends. A friend of hers once said that Dolley was bubbly and beautiful and "spilled sunshine" wherever she went.

Dolley encouraged the women of Washington to get involved in politics. She and other women would regularly attend the House debates. Enjoying the public and the life that goes with being the President's wife, Dolley would always be present at Madison's speeches. And it was clear she had an adoring public.

During Madison's presidency, Great Britain continued to seize American ships and to blockade American harbors. The U.S. government decided to act. On June 18, 1812, President Madison signed a declaration of war. The odds were against the United States. First of all, Great Britain was the greatest seapower of the time, numbering more than seven hundred warships. Secondly, the United States was divided over this war. The Federalists in the northeast opposed it and called the War of 1812 "Mr. Madison's War." The American ships, however, did well at sea and on the Great Lakes. Unfortunately, the land battles were not as successful.

During this time, Dolley tried to keep up public confidence. She continued to entertain and main-

June 23, 1812: The first naval action in the War of 1812 off New London, Connecticut.

tained her daily routines. She even gave small speeches lending support to the American soldiers. Dolley tried not to let the public see that she was worried. The British had warned the Americans that they planned to destroy Washington, D.C., as revenge for the American destruction of Parliament buildings in Toronto. The question was when. Washington waited with mounting fear.

In August 1814, two years after James Madison was re-elected president, British troops descended upon the capital city. Though terrified, Dolley had been prepared. Before Madison left to be with his troops, he told Dolley to pack important documents and be ready to leave Washington at a moment's notice. It was feared the British would set fire to Washington, D.C., and its public buildings. The Declaration of Independence, the Constitution, along with the silver, and some draperies, were among the items Dolley hurriedly packed. While doing this, she made sure dinner was prepared and the table set in case Madison and his men returned. She was nervous, though. Dolley kept running back and forth to the attic where she watched with binoculars the streets of Washington. Soldiers were roaming around as families threw personal items into wagons and began leaving the city. Dolley desperately hoped to see Madison come riding back to the President's

As the British came close, Dolley salvaged what she could from the President's House.

House. She was worried more for him and her country than she was for herself, though it was rumored that the British admiral was planning on taking Dolley hostage.

Dolley was warned several times to get out of the President's House and flee the city. The British were near. Dolley didn't leave, however, until she finally got word from James. Before she fled, she insisted on saving the huge portrait of George Washington that hung in the dining room.

The famous portrait of George Washington that Dolley saved from the advancing British.

British soldiers set fire to Washington in 1814.

Unfortunately the frame containing the picture was so heavy that it had been nailed to the wall. Dolley insisted the portrait be cut out of the frame. For safe keeping, the portrait was given to two men from New York. Waiting until the last possible moment, Dolley and her maid, Sukey, finally left the President's House.

Hours later, the British stormed into Washington. They burned public buildings including the Capitol building. They didn't stop until they reached the President's House. There they ate the meal that had been set out for Madison, and afterwards, they left the house in ashes.

Dolley safely escaped the capital city. After stopping at various homes along the way in search of Madison, being turned down at one inn because the owner was upset that her husband was fighting in this war, Dolley and Sukey found a haven at Wiley's Tavern. It was here that James found her more than twenty-four hours later. But soon he had to leave her, and Dolley was once again concerned for his safety.

The day after the British set Washington ablaze, a fierce hurricane swept the city. The fearful British ran before the high winds and heavy rain storm. Two days later, Dolley made her way back to Washington. So she would not draw attention to herself and risk capture, she disguised herself as a country woman and traveled in an old farm wagon. When she and her driver reached the ferry to cross the Potomac River, the officer refused to take them. He didn't recognize Dolley in her disguise. When he finally realized who she was, he was very apologetic and offered to take them across. After viewing the horrendous destruction of the President's House, Dolley went to her sister Anna Cutt's house. Madison met her shortly thereafter.

Eventually, American troops began to win some land battles against the British. It was the battle at Fort McHenry in Baltimore that inspired a young lawyer, Francis Scott Key, to write the "Star Spangled Banner." Dolley had been instrumental in persuading Madison to send someone aboard a British ship to try to obtain the release of a Dr. William Beanes. It was Key who was sent. As he watched the American forces withstand a British assault, Key saw that at the "dawn's early light," the "flag was still there." He wrote down his jubilant feelings on some paper he

September 13, 1814: The British fleet bombards Fort McHenry, near Baltimore, inspiring Francis Scott Key to write "The Star Spangled Banner."

had in his pocket. Little did he know that these words later put to the music from an English ballad would become his country's national anthem.

The war continued until news came of a treaty signed by Great Britain and the United States at Ghent on December 24, 1814. For the second time in Dolley's life, Great Britain recognized the United States as an independent nation, and friendly relations between the two countries resumed.

Rebuilding the capital city was a big job. Architect Benjamin Latrobe was asked to plan the layout and to supervise the reconstruction of the President's House. The outer walls still stood, though the inside was totally destroyed. The outside was painted white. This is how the President's House came to be called the White House. The building, however, was not restored until after Madison's term was over. Dolley and James moved into a lovely home known as Octagon House. Meanwhile, the rest of Washington, D.C., was also being reconstructed. To rebuild the Library of Congress, Thomas Jefferson sold thousands of his books to the government. The Capitol building was refurbished, adding a building to connect the two wings. Eventually an impressive dome was built over this.

In June 1815, the Madisons moved out of Octagon House because its owner was returning to

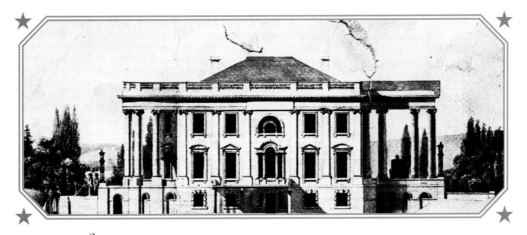

Architect Benjamin Latrobe's 1807 design of the White House (this illustration shows the East Face).

The Octagon House, where Dolley and James Madison lived while the White House was under construction.

Washington. They moved into former Vice-President Elbridge Gerry's home at the corner of the Seven Buildings. It was a comfortable but small house, not nearly as elegant as Octagon House. Dolley continued to give numerous parties and receptions. When soldiers passed by the house they would cheer for Mrs. Madison. She in turn would greet them.

Dolley delighted young children with her pet. She had a macaw and fed the bird by the window where the children could watch it eat and perform. Another thing she did for the children was organize an Easter Egg Roll. Her son Payne had spent a lot of time in Europe and told his mother of a custom where children dyed boiled eggs red and then rolled them down a hill. Dolley thought the children of Washington would love this, so she organized an Easter Egg Roll the Monday after Easter on the hill of the U.S. Capitol building. This is a tradition which has continued through the years on the lawns of the White house.

In October 1815, Dolley and many other women of Washington, organized a group to help the orphans of the city. Dolley was elected director of this association. This set a precedence for future Presidents' wives—involvement in formally organized projects. Her advice was sought by many women on varying issues, and Dolley became well-known as a leader.

A traditional Easter Egg Roll.

CHAPTER SIX

Retiring to Montpelier

★ ★ ★ ★ ★

On March 4, 1817, James Monroe became the fifth president of the United States. Dolley and President Madison left the public life of Washington by steamboat the next month. They were retiring to James' beloved Montpelier. James was sixty-six years old, Dolley nearly forty-nine. Leaving Washington must have been difficult for Dolley. She had been the nation's most beloved hostess for the past sixteen years. Seeing her husband so light-hearted, joking, and talking with everyone,

Montpelier, as it looks today.

however, made Dolley feel good. Madison no longer was burdened with the responsibilities of running the nation. He could relax and let others take over the duties of government.

Dolley filled their days at Montpelier with entertaining. At one time she had ninety guests for dinner! Another time she had twenty-three overnight guests. In those days when it took weeks to travel by coach from place to place, guests were expected to visit for extended stays. Four or five weeks was not unusual. When she had spare time, Dolley enjoyed gardening, reading, and cooking. She and James did a lot of walking and also had regular "foot" races. They often rode to Monticello to visit Thomas Jefferson.

The Madisons' entertaining was expensive and caused a financial strain. Dolley's son Payne also added to the Madisons' troubles. He was very irresponsible as an adult and went into debt several times. Madison became angry about this but never told Dolley. Instead, he quietly helped Payne out of many difficult situations.

During his retirement, James decided to rewrite his notes made during the 1787 Constitutional Convention in Philadelphia. It took years to complete the task, but he felt it important for future gen-

Friday June 1. 1787

William Houston from Georgia took his seat

The Committee of the whole ___, proceeded to ___

Resolution 7.

"that a national Executive be ___ chosen by the national Legislature ___ for the term of ___ years, to be ineligible thereafter, to possess the executive powers of Congress &c."

Mr. Pinkney was for a vigorous Executive but was afraid the Executive powers of Congress might extend to peace & war &c which would render the Executive a monarchy, of the worst kind, towit an elective one.

Mr. Wilson moved that the Executive consist of a single person. Mr. Pinkney seconded the motion, so as to read "that a national Ex. to consist of a single person, he wished to hear ___

a considerable pause ensuing and the Chairman asking if he should put the question, Doct Franklin observed that it was a point of great importance and wished that the gentlemen would deliver their sentiments on it before the question was put.

Mr. Rutledge animadverted on the shyness of gentlemen on this and other subjects. He said it looked as if they supposed themselves precluded by having frankly disclosed their opinions from afterwards changing them, which he did not take to be at all the case. He said he was for vesting the Executive power in a single person, tho' he was not for giving him the power of war and peace. A single man would feel the greatest responsibility and administer the public affairs best.

Mr. Sherman said that he considered the Executive magistracy as nothing more than an institution for carrying the will of the Legislature into effect, that the person or persons ought to be appointed by and accountable to the Legislature only, which was the depository of the supreme will of the Society. As they were the best judges of the business which ought to be done by the Executive department, and consequently of the number necessary from time to time for doing it, he wished the number might be fixed, but that the legislature should be at liberty to appoint one or more as experience might dictate.

Mr. Wilson preferred a single magistrate, as giving most energy dispatch and responsibility to the office. He did not consider the Prerogatives of the British Monarch as a proper guide in defining the Executive powers. Some of those prerogatives were of a legislative nature. Among others that of war & peace &c. The only powers he considered strictly as appertaining to and were those of executing the laws, and appointing officers, not ___ appointed

James Madison's notes from the
Constitutional Convention.

erations to have this information. As James grew older and weaker, Dolley helped by taking down his words on paper and writing final drafts.

On June 28, 1836, eighty-five-year-old James Madison died. He had been a brilliant statesman and had served his country well. Dolley once again struggled with grief and a distressing financial situation.

Congress finally bought the first three volumes of Madison's works for $30,000. Dolley received about $9,000 after the terms of James' will were settled. Alone after Madison's death, Dolley became homesick for Washington. Though appalled by her discovery that Madison had spent huge sums of money to pay off Payne's numerous debts, Dolley put Payne in charge of running Montpelier. She and her niece, Anna, then moved to a little house in Washington.

CHAPTER SEVEN

Dolley Returns to Washington

★ ★ ★ ★ ★

ack in Washington, Dolley received a warm welcome and once again was caught up in a whirl of social activities. She received many invitations to numerous parties and Dolley hosted her own traditional New Years' Day and Fourth of July receptions. Many times, to afford these events, she had to skimp in her own meals and live very frugally. Her $9,000 did not last long. Fortunately, some good friends frequently sent baskets of food to her. When she did entertain, Dolley could no longer buy new gowns to wear. Instead she wore her old ones with dignity, though they were no longer in style.

Meanwhile, Payne who knew nothing about running a plantation, was making a mess of Montpelier. Dolley finally ended up selling it. Thankfully, on Dolley's eightieth birthday, she found that Congress intended to buy the remainder of James' papers for $25,000. More important to Dolley was that Madison's wish had been fulfilled.

Because Dolley was so highly respected and regarded, she was the first woman ever given a seat in the House of Representatives. Normally women in attendance had to sit in the gallery. This was a great honor then and Dolley was free to sit in on any session she wanted.

Dolley was always invited to important public events. Samuel Morse asked her to be present when the first telegram was sent. She attended this historic event and after Morse sent his famous message, "What hath God wrought," he turned to Dolley and asked her to send a message. This took her by surprise, but she quickly regained her composure and sent her love to a cousin in Baltimore. Another historic event that Dolley attended was the laying of the cornerstone for the Washington Monument.

A Mathew Brady photograph of Dolley Madison in September 1878, shortly before her death.

Dolley Madison lived a long and full life. She had known the first eleven presidents and their families well, many of whom often sought her advice. The little Quaker girl who was born in Guilford County, North Carolina, had not only grown up to be one of the most beloved first ladies in history, but a national institution as well.

On July 12, 1849, Dolley Payne Todd Madison died quietly in her sleep. She was eighty-one years old. Her faithful niece, Anna, was with her until her death. Hundreds of people, including President Zachary Taylor, came to pay their respect to this woman who had been, in President Taylor's words, our "First Lady for a half-century." And so the title, "First Lady," came to be. Dolley Madison touched the hearts of all who knew her, and all who knew her, loved her.

For Further Reading

Blandfield, Susan. *James Madison*. New York: Franklin Watts, Inc., 1986.

Carter, Alden. *War of 1812*. New York: Franklin Watts, Inc., 1992.

Clinton, Susan. *James Madison*. Chicago: Childrens Press, 1986.

Leavell, Perry. *James Madison*. New York: Chelsea House, 1988.

Marsh, Joan. *Martha Washington*. New York: Franklin Watts, Inc., 1993.

Index

About the Author

*P*atricia Ryon Quiri lives in Palm Harbor, Florida, with her husband and three sons. She is a former elementary schoolteacher and has an elementary education degree from Alfred University in New York State. Ms. Quiri is an active parent volunteer in the Pinellas County School system. Other Franklin Watts books by Ms. Quiri include *Dating*, *Alexander Graham Bell*, *Metamorphosis*, and *The Algonquians*.